TOUGH QUESTIONS: 500 bold discussion starters

BY JOSH WARREN

Group
Loveland, Colorado

Group's R.E.A.L. Guarantee to you:

Every Group resource incorporates our R.E.A.L. approach to ministry—
a unique philosophy that results in long-term retention and life
transformation. It's ministry that's:

This is EARL.
He's R.E.A.L.
mixed up.
(Get it?)

Relational
Because student-to-
student interaction
enhances learning and
builds Christian
friendships.

Experiential
Because what students
experience sticks with
them up to 9 times
longer than what they
simply hear or read.

Applicable
Because the aim of
Christian education is
to be both hearers and
doers of the Word.

Learner-based
Because students learn
more and retain it
longer when the
process is designed
according to how they
learn best.

TOUGH QUESTIONS: 500 Bold Discussion Starters

Copyright © 2002 Josh Warren

CREDITS
Editor: *Amy Simpson*
Chief Creative Officer: *Joani
Schultz*
Copy Editor: *Lyndsay E. Gerwing*
Book Designer: *Jean Bruns*
Computer Graphic Artist: *Tracy K.
Donaldson*
Cover Art Director: *Jeff A. Storm*
Cover Designer: *Blukazoo Studio*
Production Manager: *Dodie Tipton*

LIBRARY OF CONGRESS CATALOGING-IN-PUBLICATION DATA
Warren, Josh, 1981-
    Tough questions : 500 bold discussion starters / by Josh Warren.
        p. cm.
    ISBN 0-7644-2392-4 (pbk. : alk. paper)
    1. Teenagers--Religious life--Miscellanea. 2. Teenagers--Conduct of
life--Miscellanea. I. Title.
    BV4531.3 .W37 2002
    268'.433--dc21

                                                                    2002001773

10 9 8 7 6 5 4 3 2 1   11 10 09 08 07 06 05 04 03 02
Printed in the United States of America.

CONTENTS

PEOPLE I WANT TO THANK

First, I'd like to thank God for creating humans who can experience deep and intimate relationships without having to be adults!

I want to personally thank Pat Brumfield; without him this book would not have come together. It was through our relationship that I learned the importance of tough questions. Thank you, Pat!

Thanks also to Mom and Dad for encouraging me to make this book a reality, to Ryan H. for helping me in times of need, to Matthew and Jaime for your support, to Amy and Tommy, Robby, Cathi, Jamin, Paul, Doug Fields, Matt McGill, Brian B., Barry, my friends at Group, Amy S., Dave T., everyone at Pastors.com, Bucky, all of the high school staff, and all my Saddleback Church family who I love dearly!

FOREWORD

Today our culture is plagued by superficial relationships. When was the last time you had a significant, in-depth conversation with your friends or family about an issue that really matters? How long has it been since you honestly opened up yourself on a personal level with someone you trust and care about? Unfortunately, for many people—especially teenagers—these rarely or never happen. It's no wonder that so many teenagers are lonely.

So why is it that, even when we spend a lot of time with our friends, we never get around to talking about the most important things in life? Why do our conversations stay at such a shallow level? Josh Warren believes one of the big reasons is that we don't know how to get the conversation started with a great question. I think he is absolutely right!

When we learn to ask great questions, we discover a whole new world of possibilities for personal growth and a deeper level of friendship, family closeness, and fellowship. Inside each of us is a deep longing for connection and community with each other.

Asking meaningful questions is one of the greatest expressions of love. Whenever you ask someone a question and earnestly desire to hear the response, you instantly communicate genuine care. A well-thought-out question says, "You matter to me. I value your experience and perspective. I want to get to know you better!"

5

Great questions are antidotes to the poisons of selfishness and superficiality. Instead of focusing on *my* ideas, *my* problems, *my* hurts, and *my* fears, my question shifts the attention to *someone else's* life. It's the first step to walking a mile in another person's shoes. A question takes us from our point of view and transports us to the edge of someone else's experience. As the person begins to answer, we're drawn into his or her world.

No one has all the answers or knows it all. That's why we need each other. When we ask each other questions, we all become teachers and learners at the same time, and our lives form the curriculum.

For more than ten years, Josh Warren has been a friend of mine.

It was a privilege to be his youth pastor and to watch him lead and influence others as a teenager. Every youth pastor dreams of students becoming men and women of God and then doing something great with their lives. Although Josh is still a young man, he already has done both.

When Josh was a teenager, underneath his joyful attitude there lurked an unusual discontent with the "status quo," especially when it came to his friendships. He was never satisfied with the stagnant, shallow relationships that he observed on his campus. Instead he expressed an unusual passion to connect deeply with his friends. This led to late nights that weren't filled with movies, TV shows, or parties, but with conversations that mattered. This book is the result of those late-night conversations.

As a teenager, Josh wanted his conversation to make a difference. He took seriously Ephesians 4:29: Speak "only what is helpful for building others up according to their needs, that it may benefit those who listen." Josh and his friends would think of great questions, ask them of one another, and write them down. Josh mastered the art of asking great questions—and now he's teaching others how to do it.

I can't adequately explain how proud I am of Josh for genuinely caring about helping people grow, collecting all these questions, and then organizing them into a format we all can use. I'm even more proud of Josh for being a *connector*—someone who is committed to bringing out the best in others. I'm a better person, Christian, husband, friend, father, and youth pastor because of the questions in this book and the interest Josh has taken in my life.

If you'll actually use this book with the people God has placed around you, it can be life-changing. You'll develop deeper relationships and grow stronger spiritually as you think through life's important questions.

Enjoy talking,

Doug Fields
Pastor to Students
Saddleback Church

INTRODUCTION
Explaining *Tough Questions*

"Jesus replied, 'I will ask you one question' "
(Mark 11:29a).

ave you ever gotten together with a group of your friends and wanted to do something more significant than just go to a movie or watch TV? Have you ever wished you could have really meaningful conversations with your friends? As teenagers, we often think about serious issues but don't know how to start conversations about them. Trying can seem awkward. But once the conversation gets going, people are quick to join in.

My friends and I shared a desire to grow deeper in our relationships with each other. That desire sparked these questions. We started out using these questions as discussion starters with only a few of us. But soon our group got bigger and bigger as word spread about the impact these questions were having and about how fun it was to sit around and talk! Sometimes these discussions were very moving as people shared their hearts and experiences. And they sometimes lasted as long as four hours!

I believe that by using this book, you can have the same life-changing experiences my friends and I have had. The questions in this book will benefit you in four ways:

• **You will become a stronger Christian.** Our beliefs are strengthened as we talk them out with others. Proverbs

27:17 says, "As iron sharpens iron, so one man sharpens another."

• You will develop better communication skills.
History's great men and women have been good communicators of their beliefs and emotions. Unfortunately, communication skills don't come naturally. They must be learned and practiced! I'm convinced that many of our society's problems—such as failing marriages and conflicts among families and friends—could be resolved if we were better communicators. Proverbs 13:17 says, "Reliable communication permits progress" (*The Living Bible*). This little book can get you started in the lifelong process of improving communication.

• You will be better prepared to share your faith with non-Christians.
The Bible tells us to be ready: "Always be prepared to give an answer to everyone who asks you to give the reason for the hope that you have" (1 Peter 3:15b). After discussing tough issues in a friendly environment, you'll feel more confident when a non-Christian asks you tough questions.

• You will develop deeper relationships with your friends.
This is the primary purpose of this book. The goal is not to answer these questions but to get you and your friends relating to each other on a deeper level. My prayer is that you and your friends will discover and value who each of you really is. In turn, you will become closer to each other and develop deeper bonds of friendship.

As teenagers, we all have several common desires: We all want to be understood. We all want people to value our opinions and beliefs. We all desire meaningful relationships and close, intimate friendships. One key to all of these desires is to learn to ask good questions. Proverbs 20:5 says, "The purposes of a man's heart are deep waters, but a man of understanding draws them out." How does a wise person draw them out? By asking wise questions!

This is not a book to read through in one sitting. The goal is not to race through it to finish it. You may go through some of these questions quickly. Other questions may require several hours of discussion. It doesn't matter! The point is that you're building relationships, practicing communication skills, and growing in your faith!

HOW TO USE "TOUGH QUESTIONS"

Here's a list of ways you can use this book:

- in a small group with a youth leader,
- as discussion starters with a youth group,
- to capture everyone's attention at the start of a Bible study,
- with teenagers and their parents,
- in mentoring relationships,
- one-on-one with an accountability partner,
- on a road trip,
- with a group of friends on a Friday night, or
- on a date to get to know the person or keep the relationship growing.

THE SECTIONS

The questions in this book are divided into five sections. For variety, use questions from each section. Or focus on one section at a time to fit the purpose of your group. Following is a description of each section, using the acronym SHARE:

Scripture Questions
- Explore the basic teachings of the Bible.
- Discuss what the Bible says about ethical issues.

Heart Questions
- Share your values.
- Defend your convictions.

Accountability Questions
- Talk about character issues.
- Encourage personal growth.

Relational Questions
- Evaluate relationship issues.
- Learn more about people in the group.

Experience Questions
- Draw out the wisdom of personal experience.
- Get the opinions of others.

Make this book your own! Use the blank spaces around questions to keep notes for yourself. And each section contains a "Notes" page at the end. You can keep track of when you use a question, what works with your group, and points of discussion you want to remember.

WHAT'S WITH THE CHILI PEPPERS?

As you use this book, you'll notice that each question is marked with one, two, or three chili peppers. Why chili peppers? They symbolize the intensity of the questions. So if a question is marked with one chili pepper, it's a fairly low-intensity question. If it's

marked with three chili peppers, the question is very intense; it will require a tough answer, ask people to share something very personal, or even create controversy.

When you choose questions to use in your group, consider the dynamics of the group. If group members don't know each other very well, consider using low-intensity questions until they get to know each other better.

If your group has been meeting for a while and you know each other well, break out the high-intensity questions! They'll push you to move to a new level in your relationships. Ultimately, your group will grow closer to one another.

GROUND RULES

As you use *Tough Questions* with a group, follow these ground rules for a successful experience:

- The discussion leader's job is to encourage discussion, not to dominate it or preach to the people in the group.
- The discussion leader should be well-grounded in God's Word.
- Share the role of discussion leader. Pass the book around, and let others pick questions they like.
- Some of the questions are very personal. Be aware that you might hit a raw nerve in someone's emotions. When this happens, show love and not judgment.
- "Yes" and "no" aren't acceptable answers to these questions! "Yes" or "no" answers won't allow you to have a true discussion. Always explain your answer and ask each other follow-up questions.

As you use the questions in this book, you'll notice that some of the questions technically could be answered with "yes" or "no." When you're leading or participating in a discussion with these questions, don't let anyone get away with a "yes" or "no" answer! Simply saying "yes" or "no" is not having a discussion.

To accomplish the goals of using this book, make sure you always follow up a "yes" or "no" with an explanation of why you answered that way. If someone else answers with a "yes" or "no," always ask that person follow-up questions to inspire more discussion. Some examples of good follow-up questions are "Why do you say that?" or " What do you mean when you say that?" Or you can simply say, "Tell us more."

- Go slow! The point of the questions is to take your time and expand the conversation, not to speed though them.
- Don't start your *Tough Questions* group with a very personal question such as "What is the deepest, darkest sin you have ever committed—in detail, please?" Start with a question you know everyone will have a response for and will be comfortable with.
- This is not the Civil War! Remember, you are friends;

TOUGH QUESTIONS

13

you can differ in opinions and still love each other and love God.
- If you don't know an answer to a question, ask your youth leader or a mature Christian you know to help.

Feel free to expand on any of these questions, modify them, and even create your own questions. Be creative!

My prayer is that you will find the value in asking the tough questions in life!

God bless,

Josh Warren

TOUGH

S
H
A
R
E

SCRIPTURE
QUESTIONS

These questions all have a specific biblical reference or principle behind them. The goal of these questions is to help each other grow in biblical knowledge and understanding. If an answer doesn't seem obvious, look to see what the Bible says about it. Even if everyone agrees on an answer, it's still a good idea to pull out the Bible and discover how God's Word applies to our everyday lives. Remember to ask follow-up questions and give more than "yes" or "no" answers!

1
Why does it seem as if prayer works sometimes and doesn't work at other times?

2
What is the main purpose of being a Christian?

3
Do you think the Bible has some errors in it?

4
Is sincerity enough to get you into heaven?

5
Do you think Jesus ever felt lust?

6

Do you think the world was created
in six literal days, or does the word
day stand for another period of time?

7

Does God choose the
people he uses, or do
people choose God?

8

Can you sin without
knowing it?

10

How did people in
the Old Testament
receive salvation?

9

How can God see
the present and
the future at the
same time?

11

Why is Jesus' resurrection
so important?

1-11

17

12

Is baptism necessary
for salvation?

13

Does God use faith
healers today?

14

What is blasphemy of
the Holy Spirit? Why is
it the unforgivable sin?

15

What is the difference
between thanking
God in advance and
wishful thinking?

16

Is it OK to pull the plug
on a terminally ill person?

TOUGH
QUESTIONS

18

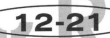

12-21

17

What is the difference between having hope and having unrealistic expectations?

18

Do you believe that people see angels?

19

Do you think that people in heaven see us on earth?

20

Is moderate drinking a sin?

21

Is it wrong to give less than 10 percent of your income to God's work?

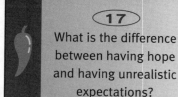

22
Is abortion OK in the case of rape?

23
Is abortion all right if it will save the mother's life?

24
When is war wrong? When is it right to fight?

25
Can a person be born gay? Can homosexuals be Christians?

26
Would it be OK to steal for hungry children?

27
Why does God create people with serious mental disorders?

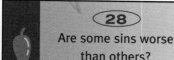

28

Are some sins worse than others?

29

Can you lose your salvation?

30

Should women become senior pastors?

31

Would God allow a war to destroy the earth?

32

Does God call us to forgive every sin committed against us, including terrible ones such as rape and murder?

33
Is it OK to get
drunk sometimes?

34
What happens to
children who die
before they're
old enough to
comprehend God?

35
Do we ever need to
confess our sin to
anyone besides God?

36
Was Jesus really who he
claimed to be, or was
he just a good teacher?

37
Which is more important:
serving Christ or telling
others about Christ?

TOUGH
QUESTIONS

33-43

38
What is the purpose
of fasting?

39
Should Christians
obey laws that go
against the Bible?

40
Does God expect the same
amount of commitment
from everyone?

41
Why does God sometimes
punish sin and show grace
at other times?

42
Can I do anything I
want because I know
God will forgive me?

43
Can God use you if
there is sin in your life?

44

What did the biblical writer James mean by the phrase "faith without works is dead"?

45

Is it OK for a Christian to gamble?

46

What do you believe the Bible teaches about Jesus' second coming?

47

Can you do anything you want to with your money as long as you give a portion of it to God's work?

48

Is there absolute truth, or is truth a matter of perception?

TOUGH QUESTIONS

24

49
Do you think Earth is the only planet God put human life on?

50
If God loves us so much, why does he allow the devil to exist and tempt us?

51
Is it a sin to be tempted?

52
Do you think we'll experience the second coming of Christ in our lifetime?

44-52

25

53

Should Christians work at making our government more "Christian"?

54

Is it important for a Christian to vote?

55

Does God have influence in the lives of those who don't believe in him?

56

Does God control our consciences?

57

Does God choose to limit himself? Could God create a rock he couldn't lift?

58

Why is there pain and suffering in our world? Why do bad things happen to good people? Why does God allow it?

59
What is the minimum you have to know in order to be a Christian?

60
Is capital punishment wrong?

61
How do you explain the Trinity?

62
Is hell a real place? Why would a loving God allow people to go to hell?

63
Is it selfish to ask God to bless you?

64
Can you commit a sin so often that it eventually becomes unforgivable?

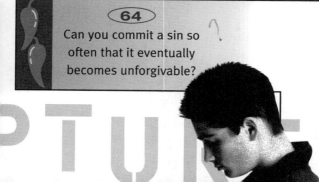

65
What is spiritual warfare?
Is it possible for people to
be demon-possessed today?

66
Will there ever
be world peace?

67
What are the things
that are going to last
for eternity?

68
As Christians, should
we accept things
based on faith alone?

69
Is there a right or
wrong way to
praise God?

70
Are only
Christians going
to be in heaven?

71
How can you be sure
you're a Christian?

72
Why did Jesus
call the church
his "body"? What
are the purposes
of the church?

73
Why live for Jesus as a teenager
when you could accept his salvation
later on and still go to heaven?

74
If you can never be perfect
like Jesus on earth, then
why even try?

75
What is the difference
between your body, your
soul, and your spirit?

76
What do you do about
activities that the Bible
doesn't specifically say
are right or wrong?

77
Is the Bible the only
"God inspired" book?

78
Does prophecy
still exist today?

79
What is biblical speaking
in tongues? Must all
Christians do it?

80
If genetic engineering can prevent
disease, will it be morally right to
use it? Is genetically altering
embryos OK if it saves a child
from being mentally retarded?

TOUGH QUESTIONS

76-85

81
Is God vain for demanding our praise? If jealousy is wrong, why does the Bible say God is a jealous God?

82
What is the difference between giving an offering and tithing?

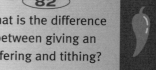

83
Do you think it's OK for Christians to sue or file for bankruptcy?

84

What does it mean to be created in God's image, and how should that affect the way we view ourselves? Is God male or female?

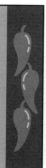

85

Are there conditions for answered prayer?

TOUGH QUESTIONS

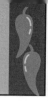

91

Is it OK to punish a small group of people for the greater good of a much larger group?

92

Does it matter if God used evolution to create us?

93

Can you lose your spiritual gifts?

94

If Jesus was God, how could he be tempted? Do you think it was harder or easier for Jesus to face temptation than it is for us?

95

What is God's view on birth control?

96

What is the purpose of angels?

86-96

33

97

When we die, do you think we'll be with God right away or we'll wait until the second coming of Christ to be with him?

98

What is heaven going to be like? What are we going to do in eternity? Will there be pets in heaven? Why doesn't God let us know more about heaven?

99

What makes Christianity different from other religions? How can you test religious claims?

100

What does the Holy Spirit do? What does it mean to be filled with the Holy Spirit?

97-100

35

TOUGH
HEART
QUESTIONS

S
(H)
A
R
E

God has uniquely shaped each of us, and we all have different sets of passions, values, and convictions. As Christians, we should let the Bible determine our values, yet the Bible doesn't give specific instructions on many things that are part of our daily lives. These questions will help you discover what each person values and believes on these issues and what is driving others to live the way they do. Remember to ask follow-up questions and give more than "yes" or "no" answers!

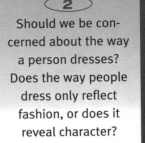

1
What are you
looking for
out of life? ✓

2
Should we be con-
cerned about the way
a person dresses?
Does the way people
dress only reflect
fashion, or does it
reveal character?

3
What are you
passionate
about?

4
What do you want to
be remembered for
after you die? ✓

5
In what ways do people live mediocre
lives? Why do they live mediocre
lives? Which of these are true of you? ✓

6
Is it OK to see R-
rated movies?

7 ✓

How could God use you
if you chose to let him?

8

If your house was burning and
you could take only one nonliving
thing, what would you take?

9

Is it OK to lie to spare
someone's feelings?

10 ✓

What are your
dreams and goals?

11

How do you feel about
taking money under
the table at work to
save your employer
money on taxes?

1-11

39

12
What breaks
your heart?

13
What makes your
heart "burn"?

14
Where do you want to
be five years from now?
ten years from now?

15
If the whole world listened
to you for one minute,
what would you say?

16
What sort of career do
you want to go into?

TOUGH
QUESTIONS

40

17

Do you feel that
God really cares
about you?

18

What kind of praise
and worship touches
you most?

19 ✓

If you could do one thing and knew
you wouldn't fail, what would you
do? Why aren't you doing it?

20

Do you think campus
Christian clubs are a
good idea?

21

If you really needed a
good grade on a paper
and your teacher forgot to
mark something wrong,
what would you do?

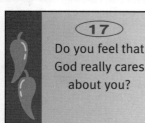

22
Does your heart match your actions?

23
Is it OK to break certain laws, such as traffic laws?

24
Is it OK to curse if you're playing sports and you get agitated?

25
Is it OK to curse if nobody hears you?

26
Should the Bible be taught in public schools?

27
Is it OK to go to parties where there will be drugs and/or alcohol?

28
What do you enjoy most about school?

29
What do you despise about school?

30
What are the advantages/disadvantages of going to a Christian college?

31
What are your greatest hopes in life?

32
What is the meaning of life?

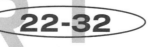

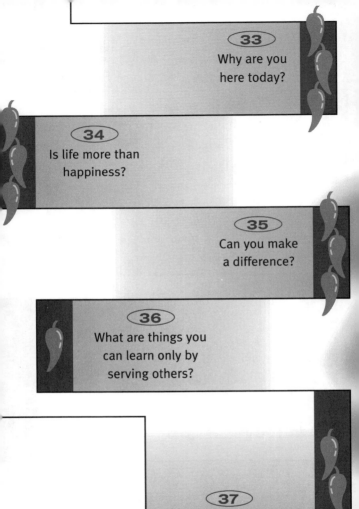

33
Why are you
here today?

34
Is life more than
happiness?

35
Can you make
a difference?

36
What are things you
can learn only by
serving others?

37
Have you ever thought
of being a missionary?

33-42

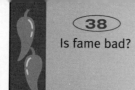

38
Is fame bad?

39
Would you consider your-
self to be an introvert or
an extrovert? Which
would you rather be?

40
Would you leave home for a
year to live in poverty if you
knew one person would
become a Christian as a result?

41
Is it wrong to
want to be rich?

42
How important is it to
strive, in everything you
do, to worship God?

43

Can you worship
God in other ways
besides singing?

44

Is cosmetic surgery
against God's plan
for your body?

45

How much attention
should we pay to
our bodies?

46

Is it possible to
have a 100 percent
pure motive?

47

Where do you
worship God best?

48

What do your parents do
that makes you say, "I'll
never do that to my kids"?

TOUGH
QUESTIONS

HEA

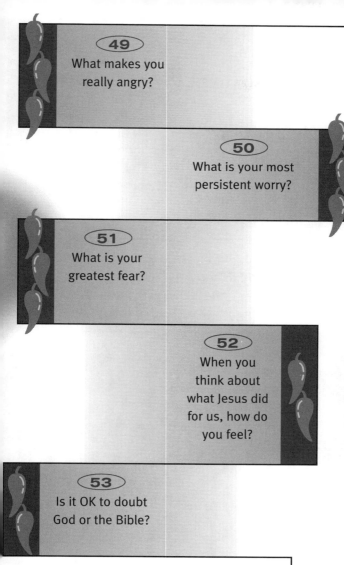

49
What makes you
really angry?

50
What is your most
persistent worry?

51
What is your
greatest fear?

52
When you
think about
what Jesus did
for us, how do
you feel?

53
Is it OK to doubt
God or the Bible?

43-53

54
How do you feel
knowing that Christ
was tempted too?

55
How do you like
to praise God?

56
Do you think you have to read
the Bible a certain amount of
time each day to please God?

57
If God called you to be
a missionary overseas,
would you go?

58
What are five
things you're really
thankful for?

54-63

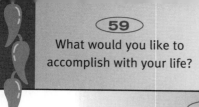

59
What would you like to accomplish with your life?

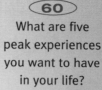

60
What are five peak experiences you want to have in your life?

61
What are some specific ways Christ has changed your life?

62
If someone told you that you had a week left to live, what would you do?

63
How do you feel when someone you don't like succeeds?

64
Is it OK to be a
workaholic if you're
helping people get
to know Jesus?

65
Have you ever caught
yourself serving to
impress people?

66
Are you a person
who holds in all your
feelings, or do you
quickly explode?

67
If you were asked to act in a play
that required you to compromise
some of your standards, would you
take the role since it's just acting?

68
Do you ever feel like no one
in the world cares about you?

69
What do you do when
you feel down and out?

70
How much money
is enough?

71
What is integrity, and
how do you show it?

72
Is it OK not to give your
best effort on things
that don't really matter?

73
Does God call us
to be successful?

74
What would you say
is your life mission?

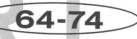

64-74

51

75
If you could have the perfect day, what would it consist of?

76
What is your favorite thing to do?

77
Is it ever OK to feel proud?

78
Are you afraid to die?

79
If a robber attacked your family, would you kill the robber to save your family?

80
Is it ever OK to lie?

81
What causes your relationship with God to go stale?

82
How do you balance humility and confidence?

83
What has shaped your hopes?

84
What hopes are harmful?

75-84

53

85
What would you do
if you found out you
had just inherited a
million dollars?

86
Why do some people
reject genuine love and
accept a counterfeit?

87
What are the benefits of being a trust-
worthy person? How do you benefit
from the trustworthiness of others?

88
Does attitude have
anything to do
with success?

89
Can you choose to be a
caring person, or do you
have to be born that way?

90
What does the word
integrity mean to you?

TOUGH QUESTIONS

85-95

91

What does it mean
to be open-minded?
Are there limits?

92

Do you consider it important
for your friends and family
members to be responsible?

93

What is your definition
of an honest person?

94

How do you spend
the majority of
your money?

95

When was the last
time you cried? When
was the last time you
really sobbed?

96
What's your favorite book of the Bible?

97
Have you ever felt what you consider to be "righteous anger"—anger at something that makes God angry as well? When?

98
What hurts you the most about the way your parents treat you?

99
In the classroom, what subject could the teacher raise that would cause you to become passionately involved in the class discussion?

100
When have you felt the very furthest from God?

TOUGH
ACCOUNTABILITY
QUESTIONS

S
H
(A)
R
E

This section contains some of the most personal questions in the book. You can discuss these questions either in a group of trusted friends or with only one other person. These questions are intended not to expose weakness but to challenge and encourage personal growth. We all need accountability to keep us on track in our relationships with God. Remember to ask follow-up questions and give more than "yes" or "no" answers!

What are the benefits of asking tough questions?

What do you consider to be your greatest weakness?

What do you consider to be your greatest strength?

In what areas of life do you tend to be overcommitted?

What specifically are you going to work on in the next week to become closer to God?

TOUGH
QUESTIONS

ACCOUN

1-11

6

What would make you a better
demonstration of God's truth
at your work or school?

7

Why is the habit of
daily Bible reading so
hard to keep?

8

How can I pray for you
spiritually this week?

9

What are you
struggling with?

10

Where do you feel
you're growing?

11

What do you feel is a little
thing stopping you from
getting closer to God?

TABILITY

12

What is one thing
you need to confess
this week?

13

Did you compromise
your faith any time
this week?

14

Where in your life
do you need God's
strength this week?

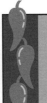

15

When did you conquer
sin this week?

16

Give one example
of how you were
stretched this week?

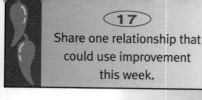

17

Share one relationship that
could use improvement
this week.

18

Who is one person
you could encourage
this week?

19

Who do you need to
forgive this week?

20

How do you need
courage this week?

21

Has God done
anything special
in your life this
week?

22
Is there anything on your mind that you need or would like to talk about?

23
Are you memorizing any verses right now? If so, which ones? If not, why?

24
What are some possible benefits of memorizing Scripture?

25
Do you have a favorite Bible verse? What is it?

26
What is one activity or commitment that needs to be dropped or toned down so that you can have more time for God this week?

27
Is your spiritual life in a dry spell right now? What specific actions could you do to help refresh your Christian walk?

TOUGH QUESTIONS

ACCOUN

22-32

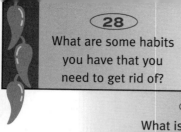

28

What are some habits
you have that you
need to get rid of?

29

What is one thing you
could do to help the
persecuted church
around the world?

30

What steps can you take
tomorrow to bring your
goals closer to reality?

31

Are you active in
ministry right now?

32

What habits can you start
now that will ensure your
growth as a Christian once
you're outside youth group?

33
What is the difference between studying the Bible and just reading it?

34
Who are you praying for regularly, that the person might become a Christian?

35
Do you have an intentional plan for bringing those around you to Jesus?

36
In what areas of your life do you find it easiest to compromise your standards?

37
Does your faith point others to Jesus?

38
What might be the benefits of joining a small group?

TOUGH QUESTIONS

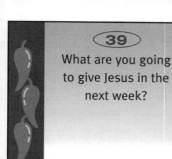

39
What are you going to give Jesus in the next week?

40
Can you give a recent example of a time you had to depend on God?

41
Where do you know you need humility in your life?

42
Do you consider your life sold out to Jesus? Would your friends agree? Would your family?

43
How well are you demonstrating your faith to people of other races?

44
What is one thing you need to learn in order to better defend your faith?

33-44

45

Do you have a specific accountability partner? If so, who is the person? If not, why not?

46

How can you focus more on the needs of others?

47

If people were coming to know Christ because of your life, would it be OK to have a secret sin that no one knew about?

48

What is going to be the center of your life?

49

What do you need to trust God to do this week?

45-54

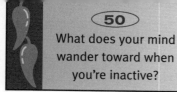

50

What does your mind wander toward when you're inactive?

51

What is one thing you would like to change about your character?

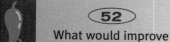

52

What would improve your prayer life?

53

Who was the last person you shared your faith with?

54

When was the last time you asked God for a miracle?

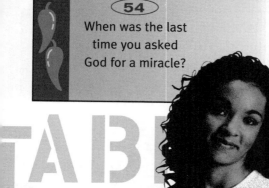

55
What is God's part and what is your part in changing you?

56
Do people who don't know you personally know that you're a Christian?

57
How could keeping a spiritual journal help you grow spiritually?

58
Why do you need to personally read the Bible if you attend Bible studies?

59
Why does God say that thinking a sin is as bad as acting on it?

60
What's one spiritual gift you believe God has given you? How are you using that gift to serve God and the church?

61
How has your walk
with Christ changed
over the last year?

62

Who do you have to
truly lean on when
things are going wrong?

63
When was the last time
you had a quiet time with
God on a consistent basis?

64
Do you talk about
your sin with someone
on a regular basis?

65
Are you involved
with the adults in
your church?

66

Are you regularly giving
a portion of your
income to God's work?

67

How often do you
do an in-depth
study of Scripture?

68

How is your
relationship with your
parents right now?

69

What are you doing to build
a stronger relationship with
your family?

70

Do you pray for the
relationships within
your family?

71

How could you better
honor your mother
and father this week?

72

Are your interactions with
your teachers at school
honoring to Christ?

TOUGH
QUESTIONS

73
How often do you pray for the salvation of your teachers?

74
Is your schoolwork a good reflection of Jesus in your life?

75
Do you stand up for the truth in the classroom?

76
What can you do to stop gossip among your friends?

77
What steps have you taken to help further your goals for life?

78
What is the best
thing that happened
to you this week?

79
Are you ever ashamed of the gospel?
If so, when? How can you move from
the feeling of shame to courage?

80
What are some of the "lessons"
that God is currently teaching
you through his Word and
through life experiences?

81
What can you do to
make your youth
group more loving?

82
Do you pray for your best friend
consistently and continually?
Does that friend pray for you?

83

What role are you playing in the church right now? What are you personally doing to build up your church, besides just showing up and participating in worship?

84

How much of the Bible have you read? How much of the Bible are you reading on a daily basis?

85

If you have brothers or sisters, what steps are you taking to enrich and empower your relationships? Do you display Christ to younger siblings? Is your relationship with older siblings really a picture of Spirit-filled community?

86

Do you place enough emphasis on your physical fitness? Does your body honor God?

87

What steps are you taking to intentionally sharpen your mind?

88

If you have a job, can your boss and co-workers tell by your actions that you're a Christian?

89

Have you maintained an attitude of awe and wonder toward God? When was the last time you found yourself truly *blown away* by God's power and could say nothing but "thank you"?

90

Is there a relationship in your life right now that has unresolved conflict and tension?

TOUGH QUESTIONS

ACCOU

87-95

91

In the past month, have you been sensitive to God's leading and prompting in every situation? When did you last leave your comfort zone to do something, no matter how small, in response to God?

92

Are you truly a servant to people around you?

93

Are you allowing yourself to be mentored by someone more mature in faith? If not, have you asked God for a person to mentor you?

94

Have you been completely honest with me?

95

Have you been making an effort lately to portray Christ to those you come in contact with, even for only a few moments?

96

Are the music and
movies you watch
above reproach?

97

Would you say your
walk with God is more of
a relationship or a rut?

98

When did you last
spend time in total
solitude with God?

99

When was the last
time you sat down
and made a list of the
sins in your life?

100

When was the last time
you wrote a letter of
gratitude to someone?

TOUGH QUESTIONS

96-100

TOUGH

RELATIONAL
QUESTIONS

These questions are designed to help you discover what is good and what should change in your current relationships. These questions deal with the most important relationships in your life: family, friends, dating, and even enemies. Remember to ask follow-up questions and give more than "yes" or "no" answers!

1
How can you be
a better friend?

2
What is your definition of love? Is it
a thought, a feeling, or an action?
Is love a controllable choice?

3
Does God call some
people to be single
their whole lives?

4
Can you have a deep relationship
with someone of the opposite sex
without being romantically involved?

5
If you're going to
get married soon, is
it OK to have sex?

6
What do you think is the
key to close friendships?

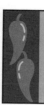

7

What is the most important trait in a healthy relationship?

8

Is exclusive dating appropriate in your teenage years?

9

What is the best thing about relationships?

10

How far is too far to go with your girlfriend or boyfriend?

11

Do you have to be "together" with someone of the opposite sex for a certain amount of time before you can love the person?

1-11

12
What is your
favorite quality
in a friend?

13
Is it OK to have close
non-Christian friends?

14
Is there a point at
which dancing becomes
more than dancing?

15
What would you do
if a good friend stole
a test for a class?

16
Should guys always
be the initiators in
relationships?

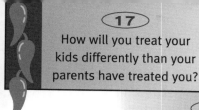

17

How will you treat your kids differently than your parents have treated you?

18

Would you prefer to have parents who don't care or parents who care way too much?

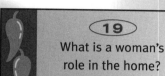

19

What is a woman's role in the home?

20

What is a man's role in the home?

21

If you knew someone was gossiping about you, what would you do?

22

Do you think your parents love one member of your family more than the others?

23

Do you believe in love at first sight?

24

Have you ever been in a relationship in which one person was more interested or committed than the other? What problems arose?

25

Do your parents trust you? Why or why not?

26

Does dating really prepare you for marriage?

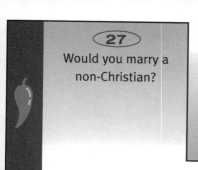

27
Would you marry a non-Christian?

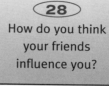

28
How do you think your friends influence you?

29
What is your favorite thing to do with someone else?

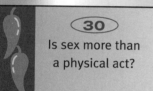

30
Is sex more than a physical act?

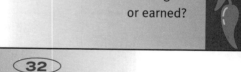

31
Is trust given or earned?

32
What would you do if you knew that one of your parents was cheating on the other?

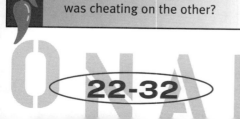

33

Is it OK to date a
Christian who isn't
as spiritually
mature as you are?

34

What is real intimacy,
and how do you cultivate
it in a relationship?

35

What do you do when
you have a problem
with a friend?

36

Who has had a deep
impact on your life?

37

What are the
qualities of a
Christlike husband?

38
What are the qualities of a Christlike wife?

39
Do you want to have kids?

40
If a friend were struggling with an addiction, what would you do?

41
How do you think college will affect your relationships?

42
Name a person you think is wise. What makes this person wise?

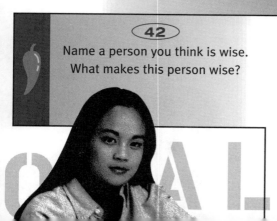

43
What are the most
common temptations
among students?

44
How do you feel toward
your parents? Do they know
how you feel toward them?

45
Do you ever feel
pressure to perform
for other people?

46
Can you give an example
of a time you had to
show love for an enemy?

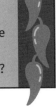

47
Why did God
create sex?

48
What destroys
friendship?

49

What is the difference between forgiveness and reconciliation?

50

Can you have too many friends?

51

How do you know when to end a relationship?

52

What is the best way to make friends?

53

Can you fall in love multiple times?

43-53

54
What should you do if you're
attracted to a good friend's
boyfriend or girlfriend?

55
What is your responsibility
when you choose what
clothes to wear?

56
What is your responsibility
when you see someone
dressed provocatively?

57
Have you ever been
hurt by a close friend?
How did you feel?

58
What is one thing you
and your parents
don't agree on?

RELAT

54-63

59
How could you encourage others toward a stronger walk with God?

60
If someone asked you how to become a Christian, what would you say?

61
What is the difference between having a right and doing what is right?

62
What is the difference between courtship and dating?

63
Can you spend too much time with someone you love?

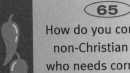

64

How do you confront
a Christian friend who
needs correction?

65

How do you confront a
non-Christian friend
who needs correction?

66

What do you think keeps
marriages together?

67

What would you do if you were a
loving parent and your child was very
rebellious and wouldn't listen to you?

68

How should parents
discipline their kids?

69

What are some ways you can deal with annoying people?

70

How is trust built in a friendship?

71

What do you do when a close friend has been disloyal or has destroyed your trust?

72

If a conflict occurred between your best friend and a member of your family, with whom would you side?

73

What would you do if your parents said you couldn't hang out with your best friend anymore?

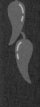

74

How can you help your youth staff this week?

75

How do you bring out
the best in others?

76

How can spiritual and emotional
intimacy be dangerous in a
dating relationship?

77

What are the greatest
lessons you've learned
about relationships?

78

How can you show
grace and speak truth
in a confrontation?

79

How can you help
someone who doesn't
care about life?

80

How do you feel when you know you've been used or manipulated by a friend?

81

What elements make up a healthy family?

82

What do you consider to be your most significant relationship?

83

How do you think you'll know whom to marry?

84

What should be the primary focus of dating?

85

What role should a boyfriend's or girl-friend's parents play in a dating relationship?

86

Is the family life of a girlfriend or boyfriend unimportant?

87

How can you be a comfort to people in pain?

88

What are the marks of true friendship?

89

Why does God say sex outside marriage is wrong?

90

Why are you waiting to have sex?

TOUGH QUESTIONS

RELA

91

How important is appearance to you in choosing a boyfriend or girlfriend?

92

What are the weaknesses of long-distance relationships? Can they ever work?

93

How can conflict lead to intimacy?

94

Has God chosen only one right person for you to marry?

95

Do you find yourself afraid to talk to the "uncool" people of society or in school?

96
What are the most
common barriers to
good communication?

97
What is the best way
to handle gossip?

98
What would you say
to someone who
just lost a child?

99
What are the characteristics of a
Christlike mother? a Christlike father?

100
Is divorce ever the right
thing to do? If you accepted
Christ after you were
married and your spouse
didn't want anything to do
with your faith, would you
get a divorce?

TOUGH QUESTIONS

RELAT

96-100

TOUGH

SHARE

EXPERIENCE
QUESTIONS

(E)

Each of us has a unique set of experiences that help make us who we are. Our personal opinions often flow out of our experiences, both painful and joyful. These questions are designed to draw out the wisdom and the opinions our experiences have formed in us. These questions can be very personal, so be sensitive to what other people are sharing. The good news is that no matter what our experiences have been, God wants to use them to help us grow and to help others. Remember to ask follow-up questions and give more than "yes" or "no" answers!

1

How do you
think God relates
to people today?

2

How do you think God will
move through his people in
the next one hundred years?

3

Have you ever felt God's
grace in your life? If so,
when? If not, what do you
think it would feel like?

4

How have your parents
influenced you?

5

Which of God's gifts
have been most
meaningful to you?

EXPER

1-11

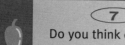

6

What is keeping someone you love from becoming a Christian?

7

Do you think computers will help or hurt the spread of the gospel?

8

How does the kind of music you listen to affect your walk with God?

9

What would you say to someone who was thinking about committing suicide?

10

Can teenagers change the world?

11

Do you have to have God involved in every aspect of your life?

12

If you don't do full-time
ministry, are you any
less of a Christian than
someone who does?

13

If someone were being persecuted
for his or her faith at your school,
what would you do?

14

How have you seen God
at work in the world in
the last month?

15

What abilities
do you feel
you have?

16

What experience have
you gone through that
could help others?

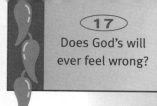

17

Does God's will
ever feel wrong?

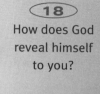

18

How does God
reveal himself
to you?

19

Should the government take a
larger or smaller role in our lives?

20

Can excessive freedom
be harmful?

21

How do you think God
views our country?

12-21

107

22
What is the difference between power and strength?

23
Have you ever been influenced by someone you didn't know?

24
Have you ever been recognized for something special?

25
What is the greatest problem facing our churches today?

26
Is boycotting immoral companies and products ever beneficial?

27
What sins committed against you would you find yourself unable to forgive?

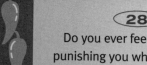

28

Do you ever feel that God is punishing you when bad things happen to you? Does God do that?

29

If your teacher were an outspoken atheist and challenged anyone to stand up for faith, would you speak up?

30

What do you do when you feel lonely?

31

When have you wished you could take back something you said to someone?

32

Can you describe a time you felt God's presence?

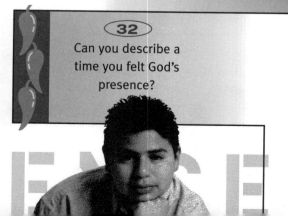

33
What does it take
to be a leader?

34
Should church and
state be separated?

35
Which is better: learning from
someone else's mistakes or
from your own?

36
What are you looking for most out
of your after-high-school plans?

37
How would the world change
if there were no mirrors or
other reflective surfaces?

38
Do ideas have to be well-
presented in order for
people to listen to them?

39

Who has impacted our world more:
Martin Luther King Jr., Mother
Teresa, or Abraham Lincoln?

40

What would you say to a
person who says,
"Christianity is just a crutch"?

41

How have you responded
when you have been
falsely accused?

42

How is your past preventing
you from enjoying God's
plan for your future?

43

Who is at fault for
violence in schools?

44

How do the
media affect you?

33-44

45

What books have impacted you most?

46

Have you ever felt God lead you in a certain way?

47

When have you had to wait for God to answer a prayer? What did you learn while you were waiting?

48

What do you like about your church and/or youth group?

TOUGH QUESTIONS

45-53

49

What do you not like about your church and/or youth group?

50

How valuable is Sunday school if the kids are too young to retain what they hear?

51

What have been the greatest lessons you've learned from any mission trip or project?

52

Do body piercing and tattoos have a positive or negative impact on your example for Christ?

53

If you could meet anyone from history, whom would you like to meet?

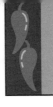

54

What would you say to someone who said, "I've tried God, and it didn't work for me"?

55

What would you do different if you could live a part of your life over again?

56

What or who turned you toward Christ?

57

Have you ever been angry with God?

58

Is testing really an adequate way of telling how smart a person is?

59

If a teacher said something very racist or morally wrong, what would you do?

TOUGH QUESTIONS

114

EXPL

60
How does high or low self-esteem affect our lives?

61
What is your favorite thing to do when you have free time?

62
How do you cope with daily frustrations?

64
How does change affect you?

63
How can you make the most of your career?

65
What are major characteristics of successful people you know?

66
Is it possible to be fully content in this world?

67
What do you think is the most popular view of God?

68
What are the greatest lessons you've learned about God?

69
Has God used any pain in your life to reach or help others?

70
How did you realize that you needed Christ?

71
Can you share a time you've reaped what you've sown?

72
What would you say to someone who said, "Being a Christian is good for you, but I don't need that"?

73
Should Christians listen only to Christian music?

74
Is there too much emphasis on sports in our culture?

75
What is more important in life: what you do or who you are?

76
How can you discover your purpose in life?

117

77

Is there any reason to carry a gun for safety when you know that God is always watching over you?

78

Is it OK for Christians to celebrate secular holidays such as Halloween?

79

When has fear stopped you from doing something you knew was the right thing to do?

80

How have you handled it when something you've hoped for didn't happen?

81

If you could ask God one question, what would it be?

82

What are the rewards for following Christ?

83

What is the difference between true and false guilt?

84

Is everything always a matter of right or wrong?

85

If you were unmarried and became pregnant, what would you do? If you kept the child and you and the father weren't planning to get married, would you want the father to be involved in the child's life?

86

Could worship on the Internet ever replace an actual church service?

77-86

119

87

If you were completely living for God, would you have any insecurities?

88

Is there a difference between happiness and joy?

89

How do you hear God speak to you?

90

Do you think people today understand God better than people in the Bible did?

91

What's one of the best times you've had with a friend? What made it special?

87-96

92

What good and bad character traits can you attribute to your mother and father?

93

Which form of media poses the greatest temptation to you as you're trying to maintain biblical standards of purity and holiness?

94

Have you ever felt like you were on the outside of a group of people? How can you include others who might be on the outside of your group?

95

Have you and your family ever moved? What were some of the difficulties of starting over in an unfamiliar place?

96

How would you feel and react if your doctor told you that you had cancer?

121

97

What is one of the greatest things you've learned from your youth leader or pastor?

98

Whose lifestyle choices serve as an example for you to avoid?

99

Whose lifestyle choices serve as an example for you to emulate?

100

When have you fasted?
Why did you do it?
What did you learn?
What was the result?

TOUGH QUESTIONS

EXPE

97-100

INDEX OF TOPICS

MORE GREAT DISCUSSION STARTERS!

Group's BlockBuster Movie Illustrations: Over 160 Clips For Your Ministry

With this book, you can use popular movies to illustrate what the Bible has to say about the critical issues teenagers face. The strategic discussion questions will get youth talking and the convenient Scripture and theme indexes make finding the right illustration easy! Plus, by teaching with a medium that teenagers relate to, you'll be keeping your ministry relevant! (Movie clips not included).

ISBN 0-7644-2256-1

Jump Starters: 100 Games to Spark Discussions

Get serious about fun with games that your youth will really love. With everything from relays to brainteasers, this book always has the perfect game. These games also prime your teenagers to talk about the issues most relevant to their lives. Games cover 43 important topics such as worship, peer pressure, dating, and God's love. Strategic questions help you guide discussion and transition easily into messages or devotions.

ISBN 0-7644-2219-7

PointMaker™ Object Lessons for Youth Ministry

This collection of 100 ten- to fifteen-minute object lessons for youth ministry is guaranteed to get teenagers actively involved. Each object lesson serves as a great discussion starter or as a foundation for Bible study. They can even be used as strong stand-alone "PointMakers." Complete with a Scripture index and a theme index, the book also includes 5 "bonus" ideas—object lessons that center around wild, outrageous objects people wouldn't normally bring into a youth room, such as cans of Spam or pets.

ISBN 0-7644-2196-4

Discover our full line of youth ministry resources at your Christian book supplier, or write: Group Publishing, P.O. Box 485, Loveland, CO 80539.
www.grouppublishing.com